Darran B

FROM
IMAGINATION
TO
SUCCESSFUL
PRODUCT LAUNCH

Simple Steps to Launching Your Product
With Confidence & Stop Worrying About
Losing Your Job

Praise for the book

"Darran Berry provides an effective hands-on guide to launching new products and business. The book avoids unnecessary detail and focuses on what really counts in successful business development. Written in an accessible style, the book should prove invaluable for all would-be entrepreneurs."

Roger Bradburn, Chief Operating Officer & Director
Institute of Sales Management ISM

"Darran's path-breaking book shows us the way to effectively launch new products and sustainable businesses. You will not find a finer, more concise and clear assembly of available knowledge on launching new products anywhere. A must read for all budding marketers and entrepreneurs."

Raj Achan, Senior Ambassador
Chartered Institute of Marketing

"Darran's book is a current 'catch all guide' for anyone looking at developing an ache of a business, where they see now as a great time to launch, and need a trusted and experienced navigator."

Katy Holmes, Marketing Manager
British Business Group Dubai & Northern Emirates (BBG)

"This is definitely the handbook for anyone looking to launch a product or service in the digital age, whether an experienced marketer or not. We've all seen the rise in gig culture as well as the continued growth of the 'side hustle' and I believe this book will give you an advantage by providing the tools you will need to successfully navigate your initial idea into a strong business."

Rob John, Membership Director
The Content Marketing Association (CMA)

"An impressive guide and very informative journey from ideation to successful launch for all budding entrepreneurs who want to start their own business. I particularly liked that any entrepreneur from a complete beginner through to an experienced business professional can pick up this book and find practical business and marketing advice that is useful, creative and innovative."

Professor Gary Smith
Head of Incubation at Amity University

"I love this book! Practical, hands on easy to follow advice delivered from a position of genuine experience. On top of this Darran gives great detail of the psychology behind the process and how your buyers think. I'm a big fan of learning from people with real hands on experience, you learn from their wins as well as their fails so that you have a better chance of success and Darran delivers this brilliantly through his book.

Buy it, read it and put in on the shelf but keep it accessible as you will be referencing it for many years to come!"

Richard Few
Founder and Chief Geek from Sales Geek

Dedication

To my wife Kitt for your patience, love and support for everything I do and to my mum … I miss you every day.

Contents

Is this book for you?

Let's see.

- o Do you have a great idea for a side project and want to pull the trigger without delay?
- o Do you want to learn insider tips about launching your product (so you can stop worrying about losing your job)?
- o Are you tired of wading through all the advice on social media and getting lost in the detail?
- o Are you unsure how to start?
- o Do you want your great new idea to succeed in the simplest way?

Yes? Then I'd say this book is definitely for you.

This short, valuable book guides you through the necessary steps to get you off the starting blocks, and offers hints and tips to help your launch be a success. Packed with practical advice, real-life anecdotes and easy-to-understand directions into starting your side project, launching your business ideas and simply understanding how to take action, you'll find everything you need to get started quickly and easily, without feeling overwhelmed.

You may be a:

- o budding entrepreneur
- o working parent
- o single parent
- o housewife/househusband
- o student currently in school, college or university
- o MSME (Micro, Small and Medium Enterprise)
- o recent graduate student

You may be none of the above. And that's fine. This book is **ALSO** for **ANY INDIVIDUAL** who is interested in improving their understanding and learning a new, valuable business skill.

I remember reading somewhere that unless you want to carry on working until the time you depart this life then you must find a way to make money while you are sleeping.

COULD THIS BE YOUR SIDE PROJECT?

What will you learn from this book?

o How to plan the perfect launch for any new product.
o How to translate business jargon into easy layman's terms.
o How to better understand the process and become fully aware of the value of YOUR "unique" proposition.
o Which type of business model to use and how this will direct business from your product launch.
o How to set up a social media planner so you know when, why and how to create and post content on each marketing platform with ease.
o How to structure the perfect launch and take consistent and timely planned actions.
o How to recognise the tactics used on social media and understand the simple psychology behind them to deliver your message in the right way and reach your goal.

How to get the best from this book

Always think about:

- o how you can use the advice
- o why you must use the advice
- o when you can use the advice.

Begin with these three considerations. Once you practice them you will notice that whenever you read anything in your life again, you will have improved your recall of any content you consume.

Who am I?

I'm Darran Berry and I have worked in Marketing, Sales and International Business Development for the last 30 years. I've been described as dynamic, commercially focused and results motivated. I'm a respected professional who has won internal recognition and accolades throughout my career and I have extensive experience of the international markets in Europe, Africa and the Middle East.

Awarded the acronyms FCIM (Fellow of the Chartered Institute of Marketing) & CISM (Champion for the Institute of Sales Management). Educated with an MBA (Master of Business Administration) major in marketing, a Diploma in Human Resource Management and a certified SOSTAC planner.

My well-proven track record includes creating and executing impactful marketing strategies, including extensive experience of launching new products and increasing revenues and profitability.

Do you need a big budget to launch a product successfully?

You may think it would be easier to master a product launch or side project if you had all the big corporate money behind you. But you would be wrong. You will never be able to master all the sexy toys out there so my advice is just to start your journey with what you have now. No matter how limited means you have available. I know full well what it takes to launch a product with or without corporate resources behind you. As the saying goes, you cut your cloth to suit your needs. And that's very true here.

Always remember that the rules of the game and the tactics are quickly and constantly changing with new applications and sexy toys that will make it easier for side hustlers to action with less resources. As a smaller business or a single person you are able to move, change direction and adapt far quicker – just like a speed boat – than a corporate or larger business who would take much longer to change and adapt to a new direction – like a big cruise liner.

Is this book full of jargon that the layperson will struggle to understand?

Every industry has its own language and the more you learn about the language of that industry the more you will start to use those same acronyms, names and abbreviations. I have tried to stay away as much as possible from overusing these terms. However, where necessary, I have explained what the terms mean so you can learn the language of the markets too.

Working through this book is the start of something big

In working through this book step by step, you will start repairing your future, thanks to the hints on how to trigger your side project and insights into what you need to consider to make it a success.

Now is the time to try new things. Not do the same thing but in different packaging.

When you consider launching your side project (or even doing anything in your everyday life) here are two great tips you should always remember.

"Everybody always wants to buy but nobody wants to be sold to." So try and make the customer want to buy by making it an experience. Forget about the selling and do it for the experience of solving a problem.

When you are next in a negotiation with a prospect always remember that negotiation is not about conflict but is all about the exercise of revealing to the other party how to solve the problem.

Your freebie

As a big thank you for buying this book, I would like to gift you something to help your launch.

Just send your email address to me at darran@darranberry.com and I will send you a downloadable excel sheet to use to plan all your social media communications before, during and after your launch.

If you would like a personal handwritten note addressed to you or any nominated name thanking you for buying the book, just let me know and I will send it to you in pdf format for you to print out.

Introduction

While there are many success stories of people launching products or services using traditional methods and social media, we do not hear so extensively about the failures. The general rate of new products failing to take off is in the region of 75 percent. This number varies, of course, depending upon a person's concept and opinion of what counts as success.

People generally do not want to read about flops. As far as I am aware failure is not listed on any hierarchy of needs. Everybody wants to succeed in one way or another; perhaps this is why failure stories are shared so much less. But this is a big mistake. From the moment we are born, we learn through hearing, seeing and actually doing. So why should failure be any different?

Cutting through the constant deluge of information we have at our fingertips has become more difficult and will worsen in the future without controls in place. Inevitably, to be able to hear, see and "do" accurately, we all need to slow down and perfect the art of active listening.

What is active listening?

During any two-way conversation, we usually listen to no less than four voices in our heads at any one time. These four voices are so busy preparing our interpretations and counter-arguments while the other person speaks that we do not actively listen to the other person.

Our attention declines further due to constant visual interferences, notification alarms and the ever-increasing expectations from people who require information at the same lightning speed as the communication was sent!!

It's little wonder our brains get so tired, and we fail to take in what a person is actually saying.

And when it comes to launching anything, we need to be mindful of our listening skills and tune into our conversations completely.

Why start a side project?

We are now living much longer than ever in the history of mankind. This fact is mitigated further by the ever-growing gig economy trend, which suggests we will **generally** work for several companies during our careers – no more working for one organisation for decades like our previous generations. The lifespan of larger companies (a company with more than 250 people) has also decreased, it has been reported in a recent McKinsey study

(https://www.un.org/en/observances/micro-small-medium-businesses-day).

The study found that back in 1958 the average lifespan of the top US companies was 61 years and now it is less than 18. McKinsey further believes that by 2027, only 25 percent of the companies currently listed will still be in existence

Right now there are more SMEs than ever. According to an article released by the United Nations, the International Council for Small Business (MSMEs) Micro, Small and Medium-Sized Enterprises registered and unregistered already add up to over ninety percent of all companies and seventy percent of total employment.

The desire to move from job to job every three to five years is accepted now more than ever. Nobody wants to lose their job, but with the rise of artificial intelligence replacing the transactional elements, more current functions will be lost, and we will all have to reinvent ourselves in one way or other.

The probability of a huge part of your skillset being outdated is high, just like that of most people. This has generated a constant demand for people to upskill and keep on learning. Social media has also created an abundance of people aspiring to become "Gig" entrepreneurs in some way or another and upskill accordingly.

Society is now taking work-life balances more seriously, and companies are also waking up to this idea by offering more flexible and personal choices.

Individuals reaching midlife and with a previously employed skillset are now rapidly being required to upskill. They, too, will need to consider the reality of working for longer as retirement ages are extended in all countries.

Thanks to internet platforms being easy to navigate, launching a product or side project in some form or another can assist in providing opportunities to safeguard against job losses and/or outdated skillsets being surplus to requirements.

Worrying levels of uncertainty in the world economic environment have always been present, and worsened by war and disease, etc. Having experienced two of the most significant recorded economic downturns, I have seen first-hand how it has become vital to ensure ourselves against potential job losses.

Don't just sit back and hope it will never happen… have a plan in place. There are going to be several ways to sandbag against job losses in your life, so why not start a side project first? From my experience, one of the most important starting points is networking with people from various business and ethnic backgrounds. Just start by talking to people and asking their opinions. People love to feel important by sharing their views - it creates a type of non-monetary social exchange for even more people wanting to listen.

Another great piece of advice I was given is always to make sure you have a healthy gender balance when you grow your networking contacts. It provides a better sense of balance for you to converse with and learn from.

The purpose of this *book*

From Imagination to Successful Product Launch provides you with a success toolbox of steps and tips to ensure that if and when you launch a product or side project, you do not fail.

It's designed for you to dip in and out of at your own pace. No notification pings … just pick it up when YOU want to.

Once you've worked through the content you will have more than just a launch plan. You will be prepared for any discussions with others about your product, and you can ask the right questions using the correct marketing terminology.

The more you learn about the launch process, the more you will want to learn. You will want to listen to more podcasts and consume more content. Just remember, however, that it is impossible to be an expert in every aspect of getting that idea to market. Hopefully, this book will provide you with plenty of great advice to know what is possible and what steps you need to consider for the journey.

What is a product or service launch?

So what exactly is the launch of a product or service?

A product or service launch is a planned and structured way to expose a new product or service to a market so that it becomes available to buy or use.

In my own words, it is the process of getting YOU AND YOUR product or service to customers in a well-thought-out way.

So what is a pre-launch of a product or service?

A **pre-launch** is releasing the product or service into the market to obtain feedback from people willing to try your product or service before its full release. This will in turn hopefully create anticipation, especially if those early willing adopters are influencers.

What are influencers?

Influencers are people who create a type of a non-monetary currency within social interactions. They have the ability to make their content socially interesting so that people care about it enough to want to tell the world.

Think of it like a bank that takes your money, or in this case the "information on a product or service", as a deposit and then uses the deposit of currency (information) to create more money (currency). Money flows where attention goes.

Step 1 The Game Plan

Everyone will tell you that it is more about how you play the game than the score itself. You must know the rules, of course, but what separates good players from brilliant ones is knowing when to execute the right game plan. It is not only crucial to know how to do something but also what the right thing to do is and the right time to do it.

Going deeper into what your game plan consists of and being open to trying some untraditional methods, you will make your game plan easier to action.

The easiest practical examples are sports coaches. They either carry clipboards or have whiteboards in their changing rooms, don't they? The clipboard contains the game plan, which is the plan for winning, and will have been meticulously designed by a team of people. The plan will be made up of attack and defence plans that, if executed effectively, should ensure the team wins.

I remember working as a General Manager for a manufacturing company where the factory and all its equipment including offices were in old aeroplane hangars. The walls were made from undulating fibre cement boards and gave off that cement smell no matter what it was painted with. As you can imagine, the roofs of the buildings were extremely high, given that the old Dakota DC3 and DC4 aeroplanes were parked there for repairs and storage after the war.

I managed to build a raised platform office in the middle of the factory that overlooked the entire production and manufacturing sections. We called it **"The War Room"**.

The War Room was made up of ten extremely large whiteboards, two for each department. Each department used one board to write down any day-to-day issues that could also be used to draw or explain points in our daily or monthly meetings, and the other was **their** game plan for the year.

Of course, all the preliminary investigative detail, findings and information from each department's master game plan was stored and recorded by taking photos when it was composed.

Each department's second board in the war room showed the results of their master game plan investigation which focused on just one or two lines for each point:

WHO is the customer and WHERE are they?

Which type of internal business model would they use to supply cut material to the laminating department? Would it be a new machine, a partnership with another department or outsourcing the work as examples?

They looked into their process and understood exactly what their product or process was MADE UP OF.

They could measure the exact goal of their department for their customer and knew WHAT their department had to achieve and by when.

Now as you can imagine there were departments such as production and quality that had internal customers like the sales department, but the sales department also had **external** customers and competitors themselves.

Board number two for each department hardly ever changed during the year, but it had to be flexible as sometimes there was a fundamental change to the department's structure or workflow for example.

What was absolutely miraculous was that each department could now see every single day what their game plan was and that of the other departments. They could NOW see that if they were successful then the other department would also be successful.

The general manager also had the same amount of two boards but had more of a high helicopter overall wide-lens view. Each department could now see the entire game plan, what we wanted to achieve, what we had planned for the road ahead to finish the game plan and finally how to execute the game plan.

It is amazing how many individuals and businesses do not have any game plan, let alone share it with the organisation's team. According to Forbes.com, more than 90 percent of businesses that have failed either did not have a game plan or had one that was not well placed together.

Important

This first section is designed to support you in penetrating the market by firstly doing some investigating into your business. The second step, later in the book, will look at the product launch itself.

TIP 1 CHECK OUT THE MARKET & CUT IT UP

TIP 2 WHICH TYPE OF BUSINESS MODEL WILL I USE?

TIP 3 LOOK BOTH WAYS BEFORE YOU CROSS THE ROAD

TIP 4 MEASURE WHAT THE EXACT GOAL OF YOUR BUSINESS IS

TIP 1 CHECK OUT THE MARKET & CUT IT UP

Answer the following questions to fully understand your product, market and what you want your business to achieve.

Product

- o What exactly is your product?
- o Why is your product technically sensible?
- o What is the USP - unique selling point?

13

- What online or offline value proposition do you offer?

Customer

- Who are your customers?
- Where are those customers located?
- In what segment are they playing?
- What is your target market?

Competition

- Who is your competitor?
- What is their unique selling point?
- What is their online and offline value proposition?

Trends

- What are the current and future trends for your product?
- What are the current and future trends for the segment that you have chosen?

TIP 2 WHICH TYPE OF BUSINESS MODEL WILL I USE?

Which type of business model are you going to pursue or use a combination of?

Partnership

o Are you going to make use of other companies' resources, technology, brand, or range of products or services?

Sustainability

o Are you going to substitute products or services for a more sustainable solution or make use of a recyclable or renewable resource?

Mechanism to market

o Have you found a more efficient or new way to bring a solution to a user?

Circular loop

o Have you found a way to turn a wasted product or waste process into another more efficient process or use as a substitution of an input?

Joining

- o Have you found a way to add your product and service into your company or another company's process that will help with efficiency, cost reductions, route to market or internal value chain efficiency?

Consumer involvement

- o Have you found a new way to make the engagement of a customer more efficient, quicker or more effective to purchase?

Integration

- o Have you found a way to integrate two products or services together to make it more efficient, cost-effective or value-added?

Financing

- o Have you found a new way to finance or pay for a product or service?

Increased payback

- o Have you found a new way to assist product or service offerings from individuals or companies to generate more profit?

Best possible use

- o Have you found a way to use fewer inputs that results in less time, better sustainability or less waste?

TIP 3 LOOK BOTH WAYS BEFORE YOU CROSS THE ROAD

This is the process of looking at the building blocks inside your company or the building blocks into how your product or service is built or made up of.

Examine what the inputs into making your product are from a raw material perspective. What exactly are the inputs into making up your service i.e. software platform, logistics, etc?

Examine how any of the inputs or raw materials get to you so you can create your product. Examine how your service journeys to your customer or what is needed to get your service to the customer.

NB: the trick to a successful business model is to always shorten the supply chain and reduce the time. Look at reverse engineering backward and forwards.

Look both ways before you cross the road: what goes into your product or service, which suppliers you use and how the suppliers or products that make up your product or service get to you. You can add more value or add more profit if you can shorten the time or cost of those links.

Additionally, mapping out the inputs of the entire product or service will allow you to be more aware and in control of its efficiencies.

Be careful not to confuse the road to market with analysing the treasure trial. We will look at the road to market in later chapters.

Tip 4 Measure What The Exact Goal Of Your Business Is

Make sure it can be measured! Here are three very good examples of business goals, however, all of them are missing key positions. Can you think what they are?

- o To make sure the brand of my product, the name and its position in the market becomes unshakable in the minds of my target market.
- o To make sure my product creates awareness as well as respect and credibility for my product.
- o To make sure my product creates prospects for sales and future pipeline possibilities.

None of these examples have any numbers and are, therefore, not measurable, so they will never be achievable. They also have no timeline e.g. six months, which obviously questions if they are relevant and specific enough.

Using the above principles of measurability I want you to go ahead and make a goal for each of the following, stating a time period of your choice for the financial objectives, overall marketing objectives, and then for the marketing objectives for each marketing communication tool you are planning to use.

Here are a few helpful examples:

Financial

Increasing revenue by 25 percent each year for the next five years.

To improve profit margins by 5 percent each year for the next 3 years.

Overall marketing objectives

Increase our market share in the UK by 15 percent every year for the next 5 years.

Increase the number of customer enquiries from India by 50 per month for the next 2 years.

Marketing objectives for each marketing communications tool

Increase our market share in the EU by 15 percent every year for the next 5 years using LinkedIn as our social media engagement marketing channel.

Increase the number of customer enquiries from New York by 50 per month for the next 2 years using social media tools like YouTube videos.

Recap

Don't be blinded by the smoke and mirrors and jump straight into using all the sexy tools that are being hyper marketed in social media. Playing and winning when using those sexy tools without doing all the groundwork first is akin to throwing away your money at this stage of your launch.

You can't play with the toys until you stop listening to the noise.

Break the process down into pieces. A customer's brain is designed to ignore us when we start confusing them. To be able to communicate our offering clearly (and without confusing our potential customers) means we fully understand **who** our customer is, **where** they are playing, **what** their challenges are that your product or service can solve and **how** exactly we solve those challenges.

21

Now you know the following:

I know **WHO** the customers are for my business.

I know what **TYPE** of business I want to have.

I understand and know exactly what my product or service is, how it is made and **WHAT** is used to make it up.

I know **WHAT** I want my business to achieve.

Step 2 What Do You Want To Achieve?

Now we will start concentrating on the **launch itself.** As you will have found out after completing the previous steps, you know so much more about your business than before. This is so very important for your overall business and product launch game plan.

TIP 1 WHAT ARE THE TARGETS FOR AND SIZE OF THE LAUNCH?

TIP 2 THE LAUNCH TEAM AND THE BUDGET

TIP 3 LAUNCH ACTIVATING PLAN

The work you completed in Step 1 will now help you place together and home in on your launch targets and the niche area you are playing in.

I now suggest you complete the next section. You might want to return, however, after all the steps in the book have been completed to adjust your lens for the target niche market you are launching your product into.

TIP 1 WHAT ARE THE TARGETS FOR AND SIZE OF THE LAUNCH?

Answer these questions:

Have you identified what your niche target market will be?

This will help you determine the best way to launch your product. You will then decide which people are going to be the target for your launch.

I heard a very good example during a podcast recently about a person with a magnifying glass. When you use the sun and concentrate the rays through the lens only on a certain spot, it will burn. If the lens of the magnifying glass is very broad and wide, though, it will not burn.

The more defined your lens "niche" is, the less competition "burn" there will be. The wider your lens "niche" the more competition "burn" there is.

The less competition there is, the more your chances of having a successful product or service.

Firstly, consider what **you think** is your target market for your launch. Usually at the start of the process people always say, "everybody is my targeted customer". This is too wide a lens to focus on and will always have high levels of competition.

Here is a good example of a niche target market. Let's use a food product example.

People interested in accessing organic foods from organic farmers, via their mobiles. Or, organic food markets for males and females between the ages of 13 and 80, based in the Netherlands, delivered to homes where its dwellers are interested in sustainability, including recycled plastic packaging and pest-free, cost-effective organic foods.

Here is a great example of how to identify your target niche market.

Take out the word "**everybody**" in the sentence of **everybody is my target market** and start by breaking it down into a submarket first, using an example of **food**.

Break it down again into a submarket, such as **organic food**, now break it down again using the prompts below:

Demographics – age or sex

Geography - location

Distribution – how will you get your product or service to the market?

Packaging – how is the product or service presented, wrapped or bundled?

Promotion – how will your product or service be promoted?

Process – how is the product or service manufactured or how are the building blocks placed together in a sustainable way?

By continually breaking it down you will reach the correct target niche market.

Another way to break it down further is by using:

Desires - eating organic food to stop climate change so future generations can live longer.

Concerns - disliking eating organic food because it is more expensive, doesn't always look as good and worrying about pests as no pesticides are used.

Obstacles - people do not know enough about organic foods, where to buy them at a cheaper price, how to get them delivered directly to their home, what kind of pesticides are used and how effective they are. Can all their concerns be answered on their mobile? Can all the products be made available online?

Make sense?

That is simply how you find your niche for your launch. Working this out will help you define your target market and could enable you to estimate the number of potential customers you want to reach.

TIP 2 THE LAUNCH TEAM AND BUDGET

Once you have decided on your target market for your launch, this will help you create a working plan and a launch team made up internally or externally or both.

Here are some basic tips to assist with a launch team

- o Get people involved (the more the merrier) who have any sort of connection to you or your product. Reach out on your social media to your friends, family and connections. Connect by sending them an email explaining that you really value their opinions and would appreciate their help to join your launch team or request them to try out your product.
- o Begin at least 2 months before the launch date as people will need to be prepared and become familiar with your product and the marketing tasks that will be required from them.
- o Form a special group on social media or a special launch team email group in order to make the launch team feel special and privileged to be asked to do this for you.

o Call the special group by a special name like the "Launch Dream Team" or something catchy and relevant.

o Give your team a free product or trial at least 3 to 4 weeks in advance of the launch date.

o Clearly explain the marketing activities you require them to undertake.

o Ask members of your team to post a review on their social media accounts.

o Ask members to pre-order the product or even buy the product for a friend.

o Get the team to share and post about their experience with the product.

o Ask the team to inform their friends about pre-ordering the product, early bonus or special introductory launch prices.

o Reward your launch team with special mentions, bonuses and special offers only for them.

At this point you should have an idea of a basic budget for your product launch, no matter how minimal. Don't worry if you have no idea just yet as you will return to this section once you have completed the next phases about marketing communications.

The best place to start thinking about budget is to decide what you want to achieve from your product launch. Make sure that you always have a contingency of no less than 15 percent.

If you have never launched a product before, speak to people you know who have or even connect with them on social media and ask them for advice. You will be very surprised at how many people are willing to assist when you ask for their expert opinion on a subject. Just remember that generally, your budget will be limited, so reconsider any operation or event that cannot be recompensed from your launch.

TIP 3 LAUNCH ACTIVATING PLAN

In order to put together a **launch activating** plan, you will be required to answer and take notice of all the advice in Tip 3. These will be the fundamental building blocks to make your product launch successful.

The next step offers many more tips and here I would like to offer an overall piece of advice.

If at any time you start to feel overwhelmed by these tips or the amount of detail involved, please remember this book is yours to keep forever. If it feels like too much information needs to be absorbed, simply slow down to your own pace until it's fully understood.

I would like to share a story with you now. It's one of my biggest learnings of my life. As the saying goes, "everybody should just slow down to a blur."

The other day I was watching some children kicking a football in a park and noticed one of the children was shorter than the others but could easily outrun the taller kids. And it reminded me of myself at that age. I was quite a podgy kid when I was young until about 6 years old when sport took over my life and I trimmed out … but I never quite reached any height really. Basically, because with my genes – Mum was 4ft 7" - I didn't have a precious chance. Frodo, me and Bilbo Baggins are all hobbits.

But I was fast, fast as lightning fast, and had absolutely no fear. (This lightning speed remains today in my older life as I can lay testimony that I am still lightning fast but now only over 1.5m.) Then both my hamstrings tear and I can't walk for 8 weeks.

My younger days were all about playing football and at 6 years old I joined an amateur Sunday Social football club called Daggafontein FC. Ironically, "Dagga" is another name for pot or marijuana and fontein is well another name for fountain so I played for "Marijuana Fountain FC".

I received many accolades as a youngster - my greatest achievement was being the Under-10 player of the year. This was one of the best ever moments in my life.

I did start off as a defender with the nickname "Killer" as I was the slide-tackling king with grass burns on either thigh every Sunday morning and I took no prisoners as the saying goes. This was part and parcel of my lightning speed of course.

The Sunday morning games were always filled with moms and dads cheering and screaming like banshees on the side-lines. Our home playing field was covered with very little grass and was as dry as a Sahara desert.

Whenever Dad wasn't working, he was there, ever hopeful that one day I would listen to his advice and just put my foot on top of the ball to slow down and stop running. Everybody else would run past me and I could pass or cross the ball with more accuracy and achieve a better result than I always did.

However, with great power comes great responsibility and this is demonstrated in my innate inability to be able to slow down. So basically, I was like a "Tony Daley" beep-beep roadrunner who could tackle like an absolute demon, but give me the ball and I could outrun everyone in front of me even with the ball still at my feet.

The adoring fanatically shouting dads and moms thought that I would just run past the opposition with my lightning speed and either score or pass the ball to someone else to score. They were always super hyped up and excitedly shouting for this guy they were watching who was so super lightning fast.

However, because of this lightning speed I couldn't stop or shoot or pass and always ended up either falling over, kicking the ball way over the crossbar and instead of crossing the ball to another person, it inevitably landed like a lead balloon inside the drinks bar across the road.

So I decided then that I was more suited as a defender. But I didn't really like it as the attackers always got the glory. I eventually found out that a winger could be the answer, but the problem still existed that I was better at crossing the road than crossing the ball.

Can you remember an old comic book called *The Beano*? There was a guy called Billy the Whizz who ran so fast he was just a blur and a big Scottish footballer called Hot Shot Hamish with legs and arms like tree trunks, known for his explosive hot shot that flew so hard it would rip the back of the net and break the goalposts.

I always thought I was a mixture of Billy the Whizz and Hot Shot Hamish as there was always that random chance I would run past 7 people and shoot the ball from outside the box into the bloody roof of the net.

What I'm saying here is that sometimes it doesn't matter if you are the fastest or you get there the quickest. If you just stop, slow down, take your own time and actively listen to others then sometimes the fastest person will speed right past you but will be unable to stop. It is not easy to hit a target at speed and even more difficult to hit a moving target if you are constantly running past it.

The constant noise from notifications and media frequently interrupts our work and we speed up to get finished as quick as possible because the next diversion is already alerting us. Sometimes taking longer and finishing in your own time is the better solution.

I also only realized later in my life that it's not just about reaching the destination, I actually enjoy the journey more than the speed of getting there and the destination itself. If the journey finishes quickly, I move onto the next destination as quickly as possible.

So, enjoy the ride to the destination because that is where the most fun is. But most importantly, don't stop believing and keep on moving to thrive not just survive.

Step 3 Plan The Road Ahead To Finish The Game Plan

In this step we're going to cover some meaty content that will help you plan a clear and logical route to help you finish the Game Plan.

TIP 1 THE PITCH

TIP 2 INFLUENCERS PLAN

TIP 3 INTELLECTUAL PROPERTY CHECK

TIP 4 PRICE PLAN

TIP 5 BRAND PLAN

TIP 6 PRODUCTION AND STOCK

TIP 7 CERTIFICATION

TIP 8 SELLING AND DISTRIBUTION CHANNELS

TIP 9 MARKETING AND COMMUNICATION TACTICS

TIP 10 ACTIVITIES TO SUPPORT THE LAUNCH

TIP 11 LOCALISED TOUCH POINTS

TIP 1 THE PITCH

A pitch is the story about the product or your business. It is the prequel or the trailer to the main event. Your pitch needs to spark interest. You need to have your pitch ready to present at any time and any place.

Here are some tips to create your pitch

1. Start with a catchy tagline - keep it short and precise. You need to decide whether you're going to educate or entertain. Create adrenalin – using shock or excitement or dopamine (the happy hormone). These are simple ways to create a catchy tagline, an example of your pitch could be: "I have ways to beat Google".

2. Describe the problem your company or your product will solve.

3. Create a story that evokes emotions. People want to buy from people, and they want their purchase to connect to the story. The story must have social currency, in other words people want to share the

story with others in their social environment. The story must evoke emotion within a person and have practical value they can take away afterwards.

4. State the problem you are solving with your product or your company.

5. Slow down when you are pitching, so you can reach the maximum absorption points of your audience.

6. Describe your solution to the problem and how it works. Also explain that it's been attested so you can give proof of its success.

7. Use visuals, pictures, graphs and facts but just remember the 8 second rule. The 8 second rule is the average attention span that an internet user has. It used to be 12 seconds but now as our brains are being constantly conditioned it is 8 seconds. So you need to keep each fact, or any slide effects used in the pitch presentation, as short and punchy as possible as this will provide the listener with the maximum amount of penetration.

8. Show or talk about your unique selling point or your USP.

9. Discuss what you've done so far with your business or your product and where you are going to take it in the future.

10. Introduce your team that is part of the product or part of your business.

11. Wrap it up by going right back to the beginning and making sure that it ties into your opening statement.

If you've completed your segmentation and done your homework on who your potential audience is or could be, you can then change your story according to the audience you are addressing. You never know who you might meet and at any time, so be prepared with your pitch.

TIP 2 INFLUENCERS PLAN

Consider getting in touch with people who you think are key players in or important to your industry. Speak to people who you think are recognizable in that industry. Ask them to try your product or service, or even just ask for advice on how they think you could improve the product or service.

Have you ever thought of talking about your product to people from the world of academia (schools, colleges, universities, chambers of business, trade organizations etc), or organizations who would offer advice on your product or service or use and endorse it?

These champions will all be influencers in some way or another. Go out and just talk to people about your offering. Talk to friends, family and ask them if they would buy or even use the product or service. Email people and offer to give them a free trial in exchange for answering a couple of questions for you.

Maybe those key players or businesses that you have spoken to want collaborate with you and endorse your product. There are businesses out there that will endorse products or services for an annual fee.

The main point is to create super fans as they will be your best influencers. Remember the money will flow where attention goes.

Tip 3 Intellectual Property Check

What is intellectual property and why is this important?

IP (Intellectual Property) protects somebody from stealing your name, product, image or design. It also makes sure that you do not, in error or with intention, copy someone's name, product, trademark or design.

Intellectual property rights are broken when a design or a creation that is protected by IP law is copied or used without getting the go-ahead from the individual who owns those IP rights.

What to do before you even think about launching!

Type the name of (and search any related words) your product or service into a search engine to see if your name, product or service is being used anywhere.

Firstly, in your country and then **secondly anywhere else in the world.** Make sure you also include the image tab in the search as your trademark might also have been created already.

It could also be that somebody else has used the same name but has not trademarked it.

Most countries allow you to apply for IP protection online in the country where you are registered as a resident.

Remember, you will pay for each class or business segment you apply for protection for. This is dependent on the segment or class of business you are applying for. Also, remember that your protection will only be in place for a certain number of years and will usually not apply internationally but only in the country you register your protection in.

Once again this is dependent on the type of IP and what type of protection is being applied for. Each country in the world should have a local Patent and Trademark Office; in some countries even a WIPO office. Make this your first port of call.

The next suggestion is to type in words like "trademark", "intellectual property" and "copyright registration" in an internet search engine within your country. This search will then give you all the necessary information about the process on how to register, the costs, how long will it take and the use of IP and violations.

The International Centre for Patent Registration (ICPR) under the Ministry of Economy is also another authority under which to register patents in your country.

If you need to know anything about Intellectual Property in detail, The World Intellectual Property Organization (WIPO) has an excellent website that can help with all your questions relating to the below topics and what exactly each term means.

Copyright - literary, artistic and scientific works.

Related rights - performances of performing artists, phonograms, and broadcasts.

Trademarks – brands, logos, marks, commercial names and designations.

Industrial design – the ornamental or look of an article such as watches, fashion, jewellery, housewares, textile designs, technical and medical instruments.

Patents – products or processes that are new and an inventive new way of doing something.

Scientific discoveries – the process or result of successful questioning using discovery into the features, processes, properties, things, causes, theories and hypotheses.

Protection against unfair competition – false allegations, acts that create confusion and mislead the public.

Geographic indications – product originating in a given geographical area or due to the place of origin.

New Plant Variety – protection of new varieties of plants that must be new, distinct, uniform, stable and have a suitable designated name.

TIP 4 PRICES

During the launch of your product or service you will need to know what price you are going to ask customers to pay. In order to know this you need to look into the following types of pricing.

Types of Pricing Approaches

Cost Based Approach

Product – take all the costs incurred to make the product plus any overheads and mark it up to make a profit.

Service – place together the cost of employing/hiring each person and what they do in your business in order to get your service to the customer.

This will help to find the total costs that are necessary to deliver your service to the customer.

The costs of all their actions then needs to be divided by the total cost of your service/s according to the actual usage of the time spent.

For example, you've designed a product that has the following costs:

45

Materials or cost of all the hardware = 20

Cost of people to make the product or cost of people you will use to get the product or service to the market = 10

Overheads = 8

Total Costs = 38

Cost by value

This is the price you think the customer will pay according to what you think the customer is willing to pay vs the actual cost of the product or service.

Even if you think the customer will pay more you only charge what you think the customer will pay. This is a good strategy if you have an accurate picture of your costs. By keeping the price lower, you could be encouraging your customers to remain loyal.

Cost of the competition

This is the cost that your competition is charging and you move your prices up and down to always be competitive. However, sometimes the price leader in the market might be using a plan to outprice you out of the market by offering very very low prices to see how long you last.

What is very important when setting prices is to always know your own costs, the cost of everything that goes in and the cost it takes to get it to the customers. Always know as much as possible about your competition and how they perform against your product or service and the most important element of under-pricing is to know what your minimum profit margin is.

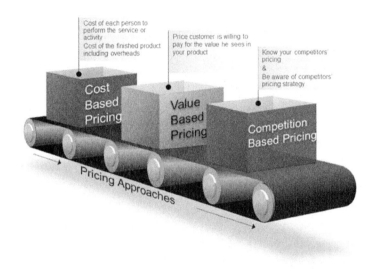

How will you charge and on what basis?

This is how your pricing will be communicated. In other words, price per product, per box or by the hour, day, month or project.

What is the real goal of your pricing?

Is the end game of your price to obtain maximum market share, survival, be the leader in product quality or just maximize your profits, long-term sustainability, scale to sell?

All these are important for you to decide before your launch.

How will you differentiate your prices?

This can be done by volume (the more they order the bigger the discount). Another option is to differ your prices by customer or their location and by the amount of competition in their location. You can also alter your prices according to the segment of business your customer is in for example education, construction, hospitality etc.

Each customer is unique and will have their own sensitivity to your prices and that is why you have to know your customer intimately.

TIP 5 BRANDING

There are a couple of points which need mentioning at the beginning of this module.

Branding is not just a logo.

A brand is who you are and what your product represents.

Creating a brand

Let's go through some of the important factors. Don't rush to tick all the boxes, as each one is important to visualize, comment upon and action. By now you will start to see some of the previous actions from previous modules being repeated. However, as you start on other components of your launch you will see that they all talk to each other, building up into a successful launchpad for the long-term success of your product.

Branding is not only Who, and Why but also How!

How is your product going to make the world a better or easier place to live in?

What do you and your product or service stand for?

Think big first of all. Next, think smaller and more concentrated. For example, what special market do you want to communicate to specifically?

Who are your customers and where are they playing? Money flows where the attention goes. What sector are they in at the moment and where do you think they will be playing in the future?

Most important at this stage is to be able to answer Who you are and Why you are here with your brand.

And now for the **How!**

How can also be called "Brand Identity" and is all about how or in what way people are going to identify your product or service. One of the biggest misconceptions about brand is that it is all about the logo. The logo is only part of the brand identity.

It is crucial to ensure that the brand identity aligns itself with **the Who and Why** as this is what will be used across all the marketing communications channels.

What is a marketing communication channel? A marketing communication channel is also known as a media channel.

Marketing communication channels are divided into Traditional and Digital Channels.

Think of your offer or message (brand identity) as being inside a delivery vehicle (marketing communication channel or media channel) driving to your customers.

Traditional media channels can include print, live events, radio, television, billboards and telephone.

Digital marketing channels can include social media, podcasts, websites, email and webinars.

For start-ups and small businesses, your choice of marketing communication or media channel will all be determined by your budget.

I found the most useful way to tackle the branding step is to create a **"Brand Rule Book".** This is a document that helps maintain consistency in what your brand looks, sounds and feels like. It makes sure that even when someone else works with your brand, it feels and looks the same. Inside this brand rule book is the guidelines for your logo, the colours, fonts and images.

You can hire a graphic designer to work on all of the above for you, but of course it comes at a price. However, trust me, if you have the money, spend it on a good graphic designer who can help you with all the visual elements to your personal, product and company branding.

Depending on your budget maybe this is something **YOU** would enjoy taking care of yourself. It will help you better appreciate the **WHO** and **WHY** of your brand too.

You can use sites like Fiverr and, for a very minimum cost, you can hire a freelancer to design a logo even in different genres. They can also create images and illustrations for your marketing communications.

Remember, it's all about enjoying the journey. The life experience is not always about finishing the race but enjoying the journey to get there.

Branding Is Not Just a Logo

WHO

WHY

HOW

LOGO

BRAND

COLOURS

FONT

TONE OF VOICE

IMAGES & ICONS

Logo – make sure the design of your logo works across all social media platforms as there are different fonts for web and print options. Your logo is always the first thing everyone will see so make that first impression a good and lasting one. Remember that the logo must work on mobile and desktop applications.

Colours – colours have a psychological effect on a viewer, so make sure that the colours you use from a colour palette reflect the feeling that you want people to have and that the colours even help to describe your brand. You can either use your own favourite colours or ask a professional for advice.

Colours communicate to the mind, emotion and body and should have an equal balance between each. Red, yellow, green and blue are the four primary colours and then further broken down into eleven possible basic colours - brown, white, black, grey, red, orange, yellow, green, blue, pink and violet.

Voice – be mindful of the written tone of your voice. This is all determined by the content and the style you use in your communications all of the time in any communication channel. The written tone of your voice determines the **personality** of your brand through writing. The tone of your voice is like the volume controller that controls how you say and what you say in your writing.

The best way to do this is to have three values as an example - fun, friendly and economical. Then take these values and decide on the style. Here are some extremes for each style Serious to Funny, Formal to Friendly, Warm to Disconnected, Bouncy to Relaxed.

Font - picking out fonts is all up to you. You can use whatever font you like, but you need to trust your instincts and decide what is the most practical for your needs. You need to consider what will work best for your brand style or the image you want to portray. However, it is not possible to say which specific font would be suitable or unsuitable - some could just not be appropriate **for your message, tone and style.**

This is where your choice of voice and style will help you decide, as different fonts are decorative, fun, romantic or classic. Remember to always have a primary, secondary and third choice that can be used, maybe even consider using a mixture of fonts.

Images - they say a picture can paint a thousand words. Images help catch the client's attention very quickly and they will immediately form an opinion based on your attention to detail and the consistency of the message through any images they see.

Ensure that any images you use are firstly not copyright protected, secondly are high resolution and thirdly high quality. Make sure the visual style of the images is in line with your style and your values. Images create recognition of your brand and trust in the brand itself. Here again, sites such as Fiverr can also provide you with bespoke images for a small cost.

Icons - if you use icons make sure they are kept simple, not too small, and most importantly that they can be clearly identified from a size perspective on both mobile and desktop platforms.

Remember to make use of your "Brand Rule Book" so you have consistency across all your marketing possibilities.

Go through the checklist below as now would be a good time to make sure that all your marketing communication channels are aligned with your "Brand Rule Book".

Website

- o Landing pages
- o Any words and structure of words used on your web pages
- o Videos
- o Any images on the website
- o The theme of your website and/or how it is designed
- o Free items given away to gather information for sales leads (lead magnets)

Social Media

- o Your social media profile and communication with your network
- o Profile pictures
- o Any planned content or posts
- o Check the style or design
- o Social media banners

Emails

- Any words and structure of words used
- Email signage and email signature salutation theme
- Promotional and special offers
- E-Newsletters

Printing

- Business cards
- Letterheads
- Any packaging used
- Signage, posters and flyers
- Any merchandise used to promote the sale of your product
- Magazines, brochures and catalogues

Other marketing materials

- Any presentation inc design, banners, theme, colours, logos
- Media packages provided to any media companies such as newspapers and editorials

TIP 6 PRODUCTION AND STOCK

The worst thing that could happen when you launch your product is to run out of stock as this could cost you your reputation.

So what is the right amount of stock to have on launch day?

You would have sourced your new materials for the first time and then produced the product for the first time. You also then have to remember to stock up at your distribution points, need to re-source materials again and then carry on producing the product again.

At the end of the day, stock is money and excess stock will affect your working capital (the money you need to keep the business operational on a day to day basis).

As you have a limited idea of what stock you need, the purpose of stock is to allow for volatility and trust me, this is the most unpredictable time of your product launch. Sometimes your stock will have a shelf life and you do not want to write off all that out-of-date stock because you were unable to sell it.

The idea for your launch day stock is to:

1. estimate how long will it take to produce more stock or have new stock available if you run out
2. work out what you think you will sell and then add a bit more as safety stock (safety stock should cover the amount of time you think it will take to replenish or produce more stock).

It is also worth considering holding slightly more stock of items you think will be more popular and less of the less popular. If the time it takes to produce more stock is lengthy, look into your entire production value chain (all the key components or ingredients that will go into making up your product) as it might be worth increasing your stock levels of the key ingredients which take longer to reach you.

There are also many other methods to consider, such as consignment stock. An example of consignment stock is when a producer of one of your key ingredients provides you with larger amounts of ingredients than you need but only charges you when you use it to make up your product. In a manufacturing environment this sometimes works very well for the company buying the ingredients because if they receive bigger orders than anticipated from customers they can turn on the taps to get more of the finished product out of the door and fulfil demand without a delay.

The manufacturer of the ingredient can produce larger amounts all at once instead of doing smaller, more expensive, production runs and make better and more economical use of his machinery or staff. This is called "sweating of your assets" or even better "amortization" of your assets. Just be mindful of shelf-life (freshness/light stability, for example) when using the consignment stock method.

Why not extend your credit terms with your supplier? This will of course increase the cost of your product initially but after the product becomes more popular you can then look at reducing those costs to where they should be.

There is another option here too. Pre-launch a small amount of product only to a small amount of pre-order customers, then you will know how much stock to hold and minimize the stock levels for your launch. By conducting this type of pre-launch you will firstly create anticipation and be able to gauge the level of engagement from your prospective customers. Creating a "shortage" of available product or a special intro offer will sometimes work and people will wait for the availability of the product. However, this will only work for a pre-launch. Possibilities exist for a full launch - you could ask your producer to only produce on-demand, weekly or monthly.

One of the most important considerations is the type of industry you are launching into as fashion, food, technology all have different considerations for production and stock holding levels like sizes for example.

For your launch, priority number one is to make sure your producer is prepared. If you are the producer, you need to have sufficient raw materials to manufacture your item and stock, but produce only sufficient for the launch. Everything else is down to your gut, experience and history which you build up over time.

TIP 7 CERTIFICATION

A product certificate will tell your customer that your product meets a certain industry-specific standard or benchmark. A certificate will tell you which recognized method was used to test your product and the testing company's mark of approval will instantly inform your customer that the tests have been completed by a recognized method and independent testing company. This is very important for the customer to see that you have used an independent source to test and you have not just tested it yourself.

Some tests are required by law to be conducted and some are purely voluntary. It is all dependent on which industry and target market you are aiming for. The best place to start is to look at your competition and see what tests they have conducted and who they were tested by. You might even find a competitive advantage over your competition if your product can outperform in a certain test.

In order to certify your products, it is important to discuss your requirements with a testing company. They will also further advise you on what the industry requires according to your product, the costs of the tests and how long the tests will take.

Step 1 Review the relevant norms for the product you wish to certify.

Step 2 Discuss with your local testing companies and send a product sample for testing.

Step 3 Test your product, complete all the relevant tests to meet the certification requirements.

Step 4 Use your certification to promote your product.

It might not be necessary to have your product tested, however, another way to gain a competitive advantage or unique selling point is to have your product endorsed by a professional membership body. This also provides proof to your customer that your product is recognized by a professional organization in your industry.

TIP 8 SELLING AND DISTRIBUTION CHANNELS

A **sales channel** is a way of **selling** to customers or the methods used to convert indications into customers or how to finish the sale to a customer.

A **distribution channel** is a way of getting your promise (product**) delivered** to your customer.

The confusion always arises because SOMETIMES the same company can be both a sales channel and a distribution channel.

Several **sales channels** are explained below. You can decide to use them on their own or combine them for the sale of your product.

Generally, when you are starting out your side hustle or product launch you will use personal selling. You will be one of the key resources as a selling channel.

Personal sales – using yourself or your own employed team of salespeople to sell your product.

Outsourcing the sales – using a third party (not controlled by you) sales company to sell your product for you.

Automated retail/service kiosks – sales through vending machines.

Agents – people who represent you for a commission-driven sale.

White label – this allows a customer to place his own label on your product and resell.

Resellers – customers that buy and resell your product, for example, online.

Direct marketing – contacting customers directly by telephone, email or even door to door.

Wholesale – generally buy in bigger quantities and sell smaller quantities to retail stores or eCommerce vendors, for example.

Retail – selling through a physical location or building.

Value-added resellers – customers that add a feature or more value to your product and then resell such as adding software.

Digital channel – this is the opposite of retail as it is electronic. Selling via a digital channel like eCommerce, a website, search engine, an app or even a game.

OEM (Original Equipment Manufacturer) – you sell to a customer who turns your product into a bigger part such as a car or a bicycle.

Distribution Channel

Distribution channels are used to achieve your promise of supplying a product to a customer. In other words, how you deliver your product to your customer.

The easiest way to explain the difference between a sales channel and a distribution channel is that you would generally use a 3rd party in a distribution channel.

Different sales channels will have their own distribution channels to physically get the product to the customer. They could even outsource and give this function to a third party or somebody else to get the product to the customer.

There are basically *four types of distribution channels*

Direct, for example, where you distribute from your own shop or door-to-door distribution. This is where you as the manufacturer sell directly to the customer and do not employ any middleman to distribute your product.

Distributing through intermediaries such as eCommerce, retail or retail partners, franchising, wholesalers, agents or brokers.

Dual distribution is when a company uses a combined method and uses marketing intermediaries as well as selling directly to end-users.

Reverse channels are when a product that is or can be recycled or reprocessed coming from the consumer to a middle man to eventually produce another product. An example of this would be recycling newspapers to make paper again.

Of course, everything works around your budget.

The first decision to make is how you are going to conduct your sales: by yourself or with a partner.

Decide if you are going to use either the direct selling approach (selling direct to customers yourself) or indirect sales (via a distributor, wholesaler, retailer, online) or a hybrid model of direct and indirect selling.

The biggest mistake people make is to place all their efforts on sales and distribution, but as you have seen this is just one part of the entire launch game plan. If nobody knows about your product then there will be nothing to sell and distribute. This is what marketing is all about. Marketing is all about the message and sales is all about the execution of that message

Let us try and provide an example of how to start selling your product with an eCommerce provider like Amazon. Amazon could be both a sales channel and a distribution channel for you, so they will sell and get the product to your customer.

Amazon themselves might then outsource the distribution to local distribution channels from the Amazon distribution centre in order to get your product to the customer and to reach destinations as quickly as possible.

How to start selling on Amazon as an example

Before you start you need to consider the following and be able to take the action explained below.

1. Selling game plan

Do you own the brand of the product and manufacture yourself?

Are you sourcing a product to sell under your own unique label?

Are you just re-selling popular products that are already available and that you have sourced?

2. Delivery game plan

If you have no large warehousing facility that can store and move goods out very quickly within 1 day then I suggest going with Amazon and taking up the offer of FBA – Fulfilment by Amazon.

You will send your product in larger quantities to Amazon fulfilment centres located close to your customers around the world or only in the areas or countries that you want to sell to.

If you have a strong warehouse facility moving large amounts of different products and being able to move out goods for next day delivery, I suggest you use Amazon easy ship AES. A good recommendation could be to use both methods to use FBA for your top product and your other products by AES.

If you want to ship on your own and your product may weigh more than 25 Kgs then I would suggest using the self-ship option.

3. Amazon account

You can either use your own personal account or create a new seller account, but you will need:

a. a business email address, and contact telephone number

b. an identification number for the applicable country you are applying from

c. a business trade licence

d. individuals will need to supply a recent bank account, utility bill and credit card statement

e. most importantly, a bank account where the money can be sent from the sales of your product.

4. Add your product

The products you can sell on Amazon depends on the category, brand and the product itself.

72

Categories either require approvals to sell, some are fully open and some categories are not allowed to be sold by third parties. If you are selling branded products that are not your own, then you must have written permission from the owner of the brand to show you are authorised to re-sell the branded product.

5. Listing your product

Amazon requires a product to be listed on their seller central or via their Amazon product listing APL. Your product will be identified by numbers such as a GTIN Global Trade Item Number, UPC Unique Product Code, ISBN International Standard Book Number or even an EAN European Article Number.

The listing will then have your offer details as well as product details and search and key words so customers can find your product easily.

All this information is available under the Amazon services link on the internet or can be found using your favourite search engine.

This is just one example of how to launch your product or side hustle using an eCommerce service. There are many many other service providers you can use with full tutorials that are specific to their own platforms and style of selling and distribution.

Companies like Facebook have a service called "Marketplace" connectors. This is where Facebook connects your partner who has your inventory and if your inventory partner is not listed then Facebook helps to get those products also listed on behalf of their affiliated large-partnered eCommerce platform providers such as Shopify, for example.

TIP 9 MARKETING AND COMMUNICATION TACTICS

TACTICS are the organized way that we send out our message.

Marketing and communication tactics are the way you will be communicating your message to your target audience to make sure they hear about your product and drive them to buy from you.

Marketing is all about the message, sales is the execution after the message has been received by the customer. They are both vital for the success of your product.

The decision on what type and frequency of communication tactics to use depends on your budget and of course the success you obtain when using certain tactics to get your customers to become aware of your product.

There are five phases a customer will go through in the process of buying your product:

1. Product awareness
2. Deliberation or Evaluation
3. The decision to buy
4. Continue to build a relationship
5. Repeat customer phase

Now take each one of these phases and decide which marketing communication tactics you will use to get your desired message to your potential customer. Remember that your communication tactics will all have different advantages such as speed, audience reach, niche targeting and how it will control the message.

Product awareness – to get my potential customer to become aware of my product

- o Social media
- o Paid display ads
- o Banners
- o Sponsoring local events
- o Influencer marketing
- o Podcasts
- o Webinars
- o Freebies
- o Word of mouth (referrals)
- o Guest blogging on other people's sites.

Once you have created awareness of your product then a customer could move forward to the **Deliberation or Evaluation** phase. This will include using tactics such as:

- o social media
- o search ads

- o email
- o incentives to buy
- o calls to action
- o freebies
- o search engine optimizing
- o PPC Pay per click adverts
- o people pitching the product like a salesman

The customer should then reach the **Decision to buy** phase. Tactics that are used here are:

- o PPC Pay per click
- o email
- o website incentives
- o calls to action
- o selling by telephone
- o people pitching the product like a salesman

The proceeding two phases are persistently important as these are the phases which ensure we make a customer a raving fan rather than just a customer.

As we continuously build relationships with our customers, we must remind ourselves that the target is also about a repeat purchase and by **building relationships** this will ensure we use the correct ethical tactics to get the customer to **buy again**. The communication tactics used in these two phases are:

- o social media
- o special offers to previous customers
- o email
- o newsletters
- o surveys
- o asking for their opinion.

TIP 10 ACTIVITIES TO SUPPORT THE LAUNCH

Let's split this into internal and external co-operation, as the main target here is to promote and raise awareness for and demonstrate confidence in your product.

Internal

You must inform every person about the new product even if they will or will not have any interactions with potential and actual customers. Make sure you have established an internal communications channel such as email or face-to-face to inform everyone about the launch and date of a new product.

Have you developed any product training content or trained all your internal staff on the product offering including any pricing frameworks? You can check your employees' knowledge by testing a small group.

Has the decision been made as to which supporting materials you or your company will use to support the launch, such as software programmes, question and answer guides, brochures?

How will you assist the above supporting materials? By using audio, text content, images, some sort of interactivity, video or even animation? This is a great way to create some excitement and motivation for everyone to participate and as a result you will now have active buy-in from everyone concerned.

When you have buy-in, you will now have active participation and when you have active participation then you have now created the most effective way to manage any changes that may occur without warning and will be able to effectively manage any objections to the product launch.

External

Now in the previous chapters, specifically in Step 1 The Game Plan, you identified who exactly your target market will be. This focused target market you identified previously now becomes even more important for the launch. Now you will harness and make use of tactics to focus in on that identified target market and create serious awareness for your product with them specifically. So make sure that the launch plan is aimed directly at your target market.

Here you need to check that all your sales channels (like your distributors, wholesalers, retailers, agents and re-sellers) have all been fully informed about your product offering. Also make sure all the content information that will be shared using audio, text content, images, interactivity, video and even animation is aimed at your target market.

Depending on your product, some of the great ways to launch are at trade shows, by publishing an article in trade magazines whether in print or online, and participating in a conference as a guest speaker or panel member.

Another idea is to place together a public relations pack that can be online or offline containing brochures, small samples, product information sheets and test certificates

You could volunteer for a podcast, write an article for a print newspaper or online industry magazine article. Sometimes your launches will be virtual and you do not have to be present. You could also organise a roadshow to your agents or resellers your product - travel to them, target specific customer groups and promote and launch your product locally.

Promote your launch event to your identified influencers and introduce your product for the first time.

81

Make sure that they know the official product launch date.

If you are using cross-promotional awareness - such as your product being launched with or in combination with another product or service – check that the other party and their sales force are also fully aware of the product and its unique selling points.

Here are some handy hints and checkpoints to make sure that your activities will be ready to support your launch.

Your Website

Make sure everything you communicate can be read via mobile devices and the format suits both desktop and mobile use.

- o Make sure your website communicates the correct message that reflects your brand. This includes checking all the items detailed in Tip 3: branding, colours, font, tone of the words used and logo.

- First impressions count … the "About page" on your website is very important as customers always want to know more about the business and the person behind it so they can relate to them or strive towards being like them.

- Start blogging – write down your own opinions and experiences in an article-like format on your website. Make sure your social media communication links back to the blog on your website, encourage guests to leave comments on your blog and also ask if you can be a guest blogger on their website.

- Remember to pull and push your content and reuse it in different ways. For example, when you have created a certain amount of blog posts you could turn it into a small book.

- Start to create a monthly calendar which plans what content you are going to create (or have already created) and what communication tactics and channels you are going to use to ensure your audience sees it.

Sonic Boom

Ever overheard or read about a "Sonic Boom"? Sometimes referred to as "sonic triggers" or "sonic branding", it is called a "boom" or a "trigger" because they are spurs which direct us to perform a certain bodily action or help us to remember a memory or an emotional state.

Think of a notification sound from your mobile phone. You know it is a message even when you cannot see the screen. Think of the famous sonic triggers like the Nokia brand noise, the McDonald's jingle or the sound of your computer or phone closing down. Those are all sonic booms or triggers that you come to recognize which evoke a certain action or memory.

I am sure you have responded to a sonic trigger in the past few minutes.

So ask yourself the question … what does your brand sound like on your website or on any auditory marketing you use?

A good sonic boom or trigger will always get a listener's attention as sound always triggers emotions better than visuals. Your own experiences whether past or present, as well as what you personally associate with that short sonic trigger will play a big factor.

Think about when we listen to music or an advert and we only remember the chorus or certain parts. You remember the most catchy parts first as these have evoked in you a memory or bodily reaction either to dance, hum or sing to. It may even have changed your mood.

When we listen to music or a jingle it gets related back to a stored moment by recalling the actual memory and extending that story. Certain parts of the song will evoke different stories or memories.

So why not add a short sonic boom or trigger on to your website, a call to action or special offer to evoke a recalled memory or even create a new memory? Be careful however, that you create your own sonic trigger and do not infringe any copyright laws by using sonic booms and songs from other people. Be original.

Search Engine Optimization

o Use the most popular search engine to see what happens when you enter your product name or type. Which page does it rank – ie where is it seen on the search engine, do you have to scroll down lots of pages to find it or is it on page 1? Try comparing your website and ranking to your competitors.

o One of the key factors for improving your ranking on search engines is to make sure the most popular keywords are used amongst your marketing content such as on your website. There are many keyword planners available to use for free on the internet, but the most popular search engine provider can also help you with its Google Keyword Planner tool.

- o There are many SEO tools available that will help improve your content over time. I suggest trying the easiest ones to understand first of all, such as Google Analytics, so you can see how you are performing against competitors, for example.

Social Media

- o Make sure your branding is the same throughout each of your social media platforms. Rember to refer back to your Branding Rule book for the tone of voice, colours, fonts etc.

- o Depending on your type of product, who your target market is and their demographics, focus all your marketing efforts on one social media platform until you get it right. From personal experience, I find that when working Business to Business (B2B), Linkedin is really popular and for Business to Consumer (B2C) or small micro-businesses, Facebook is an ideal starting point.

o Social media is all about engaging with people and having a conversation with an audience. Aim to supply information that will assist people to take them to a place or solve a problem. Volunteer to be a guest on a podcast and be interviewed about a topic or even your product launch.

o Just like your monthly content calendar, also include the timing of when, what and how you are going to post on social media.

o Using video on any social media to support your launch and product is an absolute must in present times, especially coupled with captions. People like to read and see content on the move and do not always have the opportunity to listen. So what is or has been stopping you? Are you worried about how you sound on video? Does your own voice sound great inside your head but not the same outside? Your voice will always sound different inside your head because the lower pitched tones you generate travel through your body and bones easier than through the air in front of your mouth.

My first suggestion is to record yourself and then listen back to see what the sound of your voice is like from the outside of your head and the front of your mouth.

Here are a few tips to help you on your way:

1. **Verbal fillers** such as err, erm, like, I told you so or you know what I mean are all verbal fillers that should be avoided.

2. **One-2-one** - when you are talking to an audience, start by concentrating on one person only. Once you settle into your presentation or interview then move around the room and concentrate on other people in the audience. Talk as if you're just talking to that person only and not to the wider audience.

3. **Pause** - a pause is always acceptable to wet your palate but a long interval should be avoided. A pause can be a powerful tool in your

talk when you want to emphasize a point or contemplate a question.

4. **Nerves** - when you are nervous your mouth gets dry and the speed of your speech naturally increases. Slow down or have a sip of water as this will take the nerves away and naturally slow down your speech.

5. **Accent** - if you have a thick international regional accent it's always better to accentuate every syllable of your speech as this will naturally slow you down and improve listeners' understanding.

6. **Pitch** - the pitch of your voice is very important. It should be lower than your normal speech not down to the very lowest base level but just below your normal speed pattern.

7. What happens when you lower your voice is that you become more in control of your breathing, the oxygen fills up your diaphragm, and when you lower your voice you can actually forcibly push the air out which controls and slows down your speech.

8. **Modulation** - the modulation of the voice is also very essential, it should move up and down to accentuate and express. A monotone voice quickly becomes boring and people switch off.

Email Marketing

o You can choose an email marketing platform or just do it yourself. The best way to gather emails is to offer something for free or discounted inside your website content for signing up. Make sure to promote this type of content in as many places as possible to grow that list of emails you want.

o Use the analytics tools within the email marketing platform to see who opened your email messages, who didn't, and who clicked to go further.

o Start an email newsletter. Make sure to use or design a template with your correct branding as this will make sure your branding is consistent on each newsletter you send.

TIP 11 LOCALIZED TOUCH POINTS

The importance of local touchpoints cannot be discounted. Creating a form of local customer experience which involves a local touchpoint which a person can easily relate to has become more and more valuable.

People love to buy but they don't like to be sold to. If they feel they are not being sold to they will emotionally attach their local experience to your product instead of what you tell them to emotionally attach to.

This experience is all complemented by providing that local touchpoint, in other words, somewhere that the customer can touch and feel the product. This can be done by providing small free samples. I am sure everyone will remember the small toothpaste samples that were given away some years ago.

I remember launching three different niche products into the market all at the same time. The entire launch plan was built up over a six to eight month period, and the final execution occurred at one of the largest trade shows in the world. When there is so much competition you really must create an experience that is much more than just a display. Visitors want to see and touch, that is why we created a local experience touchpoint on the stand itself.

One of the products needed to demonstrate sustainability by saving water and so we built a display using a shower head that dripped water and fell onto a porous surface. Then using a hidden water pump we pumped the same water back into the shower head again to drip down. The top of the display only was viewed through a see-through Perspex casing around all the sides where people could physically see, and yes, most importantly, touch the water. The display was strategically placed on the corner of the stand so there would be traffic from two directions.

It was absolutely amazing to see how many people stopped and touched the water on the display and in turn asked where they could get this branded product. We complemented this further with a floor display of the same surface which people could actually walk on. By feeling what it was like to walk on this surface, we again created a local touchpoint experience.

I always like to use the saying "look both ways before you cross the road". What this means in this context is do not just look in one direction for your product. Also look in another direction that might lead to complementing another of your products or create an opportunity for another product to be developed.

In this instance, we built another adjacent floor display from a totally different product and made it possible to walk and also jump on. This product was not focused on sustainability but more on bodily energy saving and safety. This immediately created not only a comparative experience in the minds of visitors, but as they were not in the same niche it attracted people to another product and vice versa.

After the show we ascertained that this display was one of the most memorable things that people took from the show that year, all because of all these simple local touchpoints.

It is well known that when people experience the product or have an experience with a product that they need to tell someone about it. Take a child's art, for example, as soon as they are finished they immediately want to show someone and tell them about it.

Also, remember that when people tell others about their experience they will always exaggerate the story to make it more interesting like the fisherman and the size of the fish that got away. It makes the story more interesting for people. This all stems from their experience of touching and feeling the product. So make sure you provide these experiences with a local touchpoint.

One final general tip for Step 3 is to remember that when creating a product launch marketing game plan, make sure it also includes a **separate digital product launch marketing game plan**. The overall product launch marketing game plan must therefore include **both an offline and online** plan.

For example, think about the social media communication tools **inside** your digital marketing game plans, such as Facebook or Linkedin. This game plan has to include a social media planner with the timings of **what** type, methods and content you will need to complete before the launch.

There are many reasons to separate the two game plans but they must **talk and be aligned with each other's plans** as the content you create for offline marketing could and should also be used for online.

Here is a basic example showing the need for a marketing type game plan for every activity (both offline and online) and their timings. Take this one level up and you can see that every marketing activity in your launch campaign needs to be included in an overall marketing roadmap with the time they need to be completed by.

Let's assume you have received a **certification for your product or your company** that will create a major unique selling point over your competitor and you now need to inform the target market as quickly as possible.

Here's what you could do:

- ○ Create a Press Release for an online (digital) and offline newspaper, remember to include a call to action.

- o Create and action a LinkedIn post about the announcement of the award.
- o Display the certification logo or award on your marketing materials, such as your website, brochures and social media profile.
- o Post a blog on your website and an article on LinkedIn about the award.
- o Submit an article on the importance of certification to a trade or industry-related magazine.

Step 4 Executing The Game Plan

Well, here we are, we have reached the most important section for you as the preparation has been done and it's all about the execution now. The moment when you expose your product to the world is the time when it can make or break the amount of bang it will have. That is why picking the right date is so special.

Every product launch is different. There **IS NO SINGLE** universal solution that works for every product and type of business segment, so be mindful of the following points.

1. Is your product seasonal or not?
2. Is there a time when your target customers will want to use your product? Your location in the world will have a deeper effect on your launch – consider a garden service in winter where it snows or a machine that picks grapes.
3. Customer's habits that are related to religion.
4. Select the best day for your launch.

After considering these suggestions, you'll probably be able to see a period in the year which suits your launch date the best.

Now pick the best day for **LAUNCHING YOUR PRODUCT** and start planning your launch to the world.

I received some great advice the other day for anybody starting up and that is to "stop thinking about the amount of units you will sell and concentrate on the average income per customer".

What this will demonstrate is that you will be absolutely and totally customer focussed and creating a future customer base who will be interested in you and your offering now and in the future. Additionally, you will be able to create a type of funnel so that you can track your client journey and turn free users into paid users.

Don't get upset if you launch a product and people do not seem to care about it. You will have to market constantly and on every platforms they may frequent. You will get rejected repeatedly and there will be plenty of lessons along the way. If you are starting out with limited resources, as I explained, forget the mass market and concentrate on a smaller concentrated market. It has never been easier to talk to customers directly using digital means.

I recall attending a trade show in Ethiopia some years ago. The show was always over a three-day period and included one day of the weekend for the general public and students to enter. What we experienced every year was that the first day was always allocated for dignitaries and government officials and nothing was ever sold on that day as the public's entry was restricted. The second day was for the trade and the third - the weekend day - was by far the busiest as the last day the vendors gave away any remaining goods from the stands to the general public.

So we decided to have one person man the stand on the first day and fully manned for the second. The second day was when we launched and demonstrated our new products to the trade. However, on the third day we gave away a product every two hours after students or the general public entered their email address into the draw. The email address gave us permission for future points of possible interested contacts. The prize was a funded set of short course options at the local university. What was clearly illustrated here was that different tactics were needed for different days and that on each day the customer experience had to change, so pick your day carefully

Of course, depending on the type of product, the amount of budget you are able to allocate for launching your product will generally determine the amount and speed of exposure as well as the customer experience you want to provide.

The saying goes to cut your coat to suit your cloth, which means we need to be flexible to our situations. Look at the funds or means you have at your disposal and make the most of them by focusing specifically on your target market. Your cloth may look different to everybody else's but the coat still has the same function to keep you dry or warm.

I launched three new products at a trade fair recently and had the budget to provide a great customer experience with special customer interaction possibilities, such as jumping and walking on a special made surface similar to the bouncy effect of a running shoe. We had a corner stand with all the bells and whistles, flashing lights, signs, videos and to a certain amount we had the budget to spend.

What we did find however, was that nobody wanted to enter into the stand and engage. What we found out was that the most effective tactic to attract people inside the stand was simply by placing a big stand-alone transparent jar of the raw material on a counter at the entrance to the stand. People would stop and place their hands in this large jar just to touch and feel the product and this brought the exposure we needed to attract them. So with a little cost for a glass jar we created the awareness and simple customer experience for them to engage further with the product.

Conclusion

We have just covered the entire process of what needs to be considered to make your product launch successful. The tips covered in this book will additionally help you to create, steer and manage your side project, product and of course your business. By taking note of the steps and hints you will also now be able to see that your product launch has been developed from a well thought out game plan and not just a hope that it will be a success.

Hopefully, you will have gathered the necessary momentum to start the process of upskilling yourself and started the journey to create that buffer against any job loss possibility. You will also better understand the entire chain of value for your product's offer and that a digital marketing timing planner is also a critical part of your digital game plan.

Summary

Here is a quick summary of the steps and tips.

Months 1–4

Step 1 The Game Plan

TIP 1 CHECK OUT THE MARKET & CUT IT UP

TIP 2 WHICH TYPE OF BUSINESS MODEL WILL I USE?

TIP 3 LOOK BOTH WAYS BEFORE YOU CROSS THE ROAD

TIP 4 MEASURE WHAT THE EXACT GOAL OF YOUR BUSINESS IS

Check Out the Market & Cut it Up – I know **WHO** is my customer and **WHERE** they are.

Which Type of Business Model Will I Use? – I know **WHAT** type of business I want to have.

Look Both Ways Before You Cross the Road – I now understand and know exactly what my product is **MADE UP OF.**

Measure What is the Exact Goal of Your Business – I know **WHAT** I want my business to achieve.

Step 2 What Do You Want to Achieve?

TIP 1 WHAT ARE THE TARGETS FOR AND SIZE OF THE LAUNCH?

TIP 2 THE LAUNCH TEAM AND THE BUDGET

TIP 3 LAUNCH ACTIVATING PLAN

Step 2 was about creating the start process for concentrating on the *launch itself*. You decided on the goals that you want to achieve from the launch by working on the three tips provided.

You narrowed down to find your niche for your launch and discovered your target market and decided on the number of potential customers you want to reach.

You have started to place together a working plan for your launch and a launch team made up of people internally or externally or even both.

You should at this point have a small idea of a budget in mind as this could firstly be all you can afford for a launch. I would anticipate you have returned to Step 2 once you completed Step 3 as you will have a far better understanding of your budget by this time.

Months 4–6

Step 3 Plan The Road Ahead To Finish The Game Plan

TIP 1 THE PITCH

TIP 2 INFLUENCERS PLAN

TIP 3 INTELLECTUAL PROPERTY CHECK

TIP 4 PRICE PLAN

TIP 5 BRAND PLAN

TIP 6 PRODUCTION AND STOCK

TIP 7 CERTIFICATION

TIP 8 SELLING AND DISTRIBUTION CHANNELS

TIP 9 MARKETING AND COMMUNICATION TACTICS

TIP 10 ACTIVITIES TO SUPPORT THE LAUNCH

TIP 11 LOCALISED TOUCH POINTS

Step 3 offered you many tips and pieces of advice. No doubt it would have taken the most time to complete out of all the steps. But in completing it, you will have so much more insight into your business, your product, the market and its dynamics and, of course, yourself.

The level of detail that you have consumed and discovered from all these tips will be an eye-opener when it comes to launching, and it will prepare you for more business and life experiences than you could ever think of.

Months 4–6

Step 4 Executing The Game Plan

Step 4 was all about deciding on an exact date for the moment you expose your product to the world.

There are so many new applications, new social media platforms and constant changes and upgrades to the current social media platforms that it is impossible to be able to cover everything in this book (and be an expert in all of them).

With current social media platforms changing so rapidly and new apps coming into the market all the time, there may be some to assist you with product launches and the successful selling of your product. There is currently an abundance of information available to you from the internet. The internet can provide you with concentrated social media video tutorials that will assist you in launching your product on their specific sites.

The big difference now is that you have the necessary insights and skillsets to easily align your product with the requirements of different social media platforms to place your product on their sites.

Now you have read this book you should know:

- how to start and plan your side project for the perfect product launch for a new product
- how to structure and run the perfect launch and take consistent and planned actions
- the meaning of certain business terminology and terms
- the entire chain to become fully aware of the value of YOUR "unique" proposition
- what type of business model to use and how this will direct your product launch
- how to recognise some of the tactics that social media uses and understand the simple psychology to deliver the right message in the right way to smash your way to what you want to achieve!

Most importantly, it has hopefully provided you with new skills and purpose to buffer against any skill set changes and job loss possibilities.

A Simple Request

At the moment the world is going through the biggest social exercise in the history of mankind and some really challenging times. As a society we all need to stand together so we can all repair the future.

So when you trigger your side hustle or launch your next project here are some ideas to consider or keep in the back of your mind. Sometimes it is all about preparing the road for future generations of side projects, side hustles, product launches or Micro, Small, and Medium size businesses.

Ways in which we can ALL help to repair the future

- o Use unconventional solutions.
- o Have a social conscience.

- o Have rules or directives that are initiated as well as upheld by an authority.
- o Gather intellect by experience, education or training.
- o Ethically evolve our choice of working alternatives for working women/men as well as a consideration for all end users and customers.

About The Author

Darran is a Marketing, Commercial Sales and Business Development specialist and author of the new book *From Imagination to Successful Product Launch: Simple Steps to Launching Your Product With Confidence & Stop Worrying About Losing Your Job.*

Currently resides and works in Dubai - that is for the moment - as Darran has travelled for over 30 years throughout many international markets accruing his working experience and intelligence gathering.

Darran has first-hand experience in the creation and execution of impactful marketing strategies as well as the launching of many new products combined with continual increases in revenue and profitability. He consistently produces unprecedented results and has a proven track record through strong relationship management.

His education features a Master of Business Administration Degree (MBA) majoring in marketing from Anglia Ruskin University in the United Kingdom,

Diploma in Human Resource Management from University of Johannesburg in South Africa, Certified Digital Marketer from London Institute of International Studies & Research Centre as well as a certified SOSTAC marketing planner.

Darran is a respected professional who has won internal recognition and accolades throughout his career and been awarded the acronyms FCIM (Fellow of the Chartered Institute of Marketing) & CISM (Champion for the Institute of Sales Management)

Darran was born in Manchester in the United Kingdom and he has relocated and travelled the world many times during his lifetime.

For most of his career, Darran has worked for European companies that have allowed him the opportunity to travel within Africa as well as the Middle East. Darran enjoyed the journey of setting up distribution networks for Southern African companies venturing many times into Kenya in East Africa, Nigeria in West Africa and even as far as Addis Ababa in Ethiopia. Darran's expertise has enabled him, for many years, to teach numerous individuals and companies how to manufacture and market products from their invention, manufacture and then finally launching into the market.

Darran's extensive career has had many interesting highlights, such as a product launch during a live TV event that featured a live demo and workshop for a rail ballast product in Addis Ababa Ethiopia. He has also been General Manager for an automotive component manufacturing company for several of the major Original Equipment Manufacturers (OEM.)

More recently, Darran has created as well as developed a full marketing and business plan strategy, route to market and sales cycle plan for three successful products that were launched and culminated at The Big Five Construction Show in Dubai.

Before You Go ...

Thank you so much for reading this book. I hope you have found it helpful and I wish you every success in your product launch journey.

If you enjoyed the book, I would be extremely grateful if you left an honest review and share and post about the book. Tell your friends if you enjoyed the book or why not surprise them with a copy as a gift?

I hope it opens your mind that anything is possible if we all just slow down to a blur and listen...

Thanks for your support.

Ciao, Darran

PS: Don't forget your freebie – simply email me at darran@darranberry.com for your downloadable excel sheet to plan all your social media communications before, during and after your launch.

Printed in Great Britain
by Amazon

60014697R00078